3rd and Goal

Great Football of the 20th Century

Mel Cebulash

New Readers Press

New Readers Press wishes to thank
National Football League Properties, Inc.
for its help in producing this book.
Philip Barber, Editor—Special Projects

Copyright © 1993
New Readers Press
Publishing Division of Laubach Literacy International
Box 131, Syracuse, New York 13210-0131

All rights reserved. No part of this book may be reproduced or transmitted in any form or by any means, electronic or mechanical, including photocopying, recording, or by any information storage and retrieval system, without permission in writing from the publisher.
Printed in the United States of America

Photo credit:
Page 16 © Lou Witt/NFL photos;
page 32 © Malcolm Emmons/NFL photos;
all others AP/WIDE WORLD PHOTOS

9 8 7 6 5 4 3 2 1

Library of Congress Cataloging-in-Publication Data

Cebulash, Mel.
3rd and goal : great football of the 20th century /
Mel Cebulash.
p. cm.
ISBN 0-88336-743-2
1. Football—United States—History—20th century.
2. Football players—United States—Biography.
I. Title. II. Title: Third and goal
[GV939.A1C43 1993]
796.332'0973—dc20   93-433
                                     CIP

Contents

Introduction 5

Opening Night Magic 7

Alive and Kicking! 14

Running Hot in the Cold 20

Hard Fought, Hard Won 27

The Big Mouth's Big Game 34

Doing the Impossible 42

The Running Machine 49

Super Bowl Superman 56

Introduction

When I was growing up in Union City, New Jersey, kids ran home after school to change their clothes and get back to the school yard.

In those days, school yards were training grounds for sports. In the winter, the school yard was our football field. We played touch football.

I remember two Saturdays well. We played real football against a real team. This team from North Bergen had shoes, shoulder pads, helmets, and sweatshirts with numbers on them. They even had a coach.

We had 11 guys. We were tougher than those kids. We could blow them away in basketball. So beating them in football seemed easy enough.

On the Friday before our first game with North Bergen, our team met in the school yard and picked our positions. The next morning, we got killed by about 60–0.

All through the following week, we practiced in the school yard. For us, practice meant playing touch football instead of basketball. On Saturday morning, we lost again. This time, the score was only about 48–0.

On the way home, we figured out why we lost. They had helmets and shirts and other equipment. We couldn't get any of that stuff, so we quit playing them.

We were wrong. We never would have beaten those kids. They were a *team*.

Great pro football players are featured in these stories, each with his own special style of playing. Still, all these players have one thing in common. They are team players. Of all sports, football is a team game—no matter who's playing.

—Mel Cebulash

Norm Van Brocklin's passing show

Opening Night Magic

A big crowd came out for the game. It was Friday night in Los Angeles. The hometown Rams were playing against the New York Yanks, a new NFL team. It was the 1951 season opener for both teams. The Rams weren't in top form. Bob Waterfield, their longtime star quarterback, was injured. A key running back was out, too.

Los Angeles fans weren't worried about the game. Norm Van Brocklin, the substitute quarterback, was also a star player.

Van Brocklin had been the Rams' starting passer for most of the 1950 season. He'd even led the league in passing. That fact alone would have made Norm the first-string quarterback on any team—except the Rams.

When Waterfield could throw, he got the starting spot. The younger Van Brocklin couldn't make the Rams change the starting lineup. All he could do was play his best and wait for his turn.

Shortly after the opening kickoff, a Van Brocklin pass moved the Rams down the field. L.A. fans cheered their great second-string quarterback.

The cheering fired up Van Brocklin. Working from the Yanks' 46-yard line, he faked a handoff and went back to pass. Spotting an open man, he sent the football down the field.

L.A. fans jumped up. It was a touchdown pass to "Crazylegs" Hirsch! They cheered as the team lined up for the extra point. The kick was good, giving the Rams a quick 7–0 lead.

Minutes later, the football again came over to the Rams. Van Brocklin wasted no time. He looked down the field once more and saw Hirsch in the open.

Van Brocklin fired the ball into Crazylegs's waiting arms for another long touchdown. L.A. fans roared with joy. The extra point gave the Rams a 14–0 lead.

Norm Van Brocklin struck again just before the quarter ended. This time, he teamed up with "Vitamin T" Smith for a 67-yard touchdown play.

The New York team played hard in the second quarter. But they couldn't stop Van Brocklin's passing game.

He even got into the scoring. First, he moved the team all the way down the field. Then he kept the ball and dove over for a 1-yard touchdown. When the halftime whistle blew, the Rams led 34–7.

At the beginning of the second half, the Yanks seemed stronger. For a time, they held off the Rams. Yet they weren't able to move the football when L.A. gave it up.

The Rams had a comfortable lead. Still, Van Brocklin wasn't through for the night. Just before the third quarter ended, he hit Hirsch with another touchdown toss.

The final quarter started with L.A. leading 41–7. It didn't seem as if the Yanks could catch up. The Rams were well on their way to an opening-game win.

Some fans headed for the exits. Others stayed in their seats. They loved the way the Rams were playing. They also were beginning to think they were seeing a very special game. Van Brocklin was putting on a passing show!

The L.A. quarterback kept finding men open. In minutes, the Rams drove to the New York 1-yard line.

The Yanks set themselves at the goal. They weren't going to let the Rams quarterback sneak over with another score.

Faking a rush, Van Brocklin moved back and found Crazylegs open. L.A. fans went wild as Hirsch pulled in another touchdown pass.

Before the game ended, the Rams scored once more. The Yanks scored again, too. They'd tried, but Van Brocklin had been too much for them. The final score was L.A. 54, New York 14.

L.A. fans stood and cheered. They watched the Rams run off the field. Their team had opened the season with a great game.

With four touchdowns, Crazylegs Hirsch had gotten off to a good start. He went on to lead the NFL that year with 17 touchdowns.

Norm Van Brocklin's passing show turned out to be a game for the NFL record book. He tried 41 passes and hit on 27. Five of his passes were touchdown throws.

In all, Van Brocklin gained 554 yards with his passes. This was a new NFL record. He became the first quarterback in pro football to pass for over 500 yards in a game.

Norm Van Brocklin set a tough record that night. It has stood for over 40 years.

The Rams went on to win the NFL Championship in 1951. Their regular starting quarterback, Bob Waterfield, led the league in passing.

Van Brocklin took over again as the NFL's leading passer in 1952 and 1954. He later went to the Philadelphia Eagles and finished his playing days there.

Over the years, Van Brocklin played in some very hard games. Many of these

Norm Van Brocklin was the first pro quarterback to pass for over 500 yards in a single game (1951).

games were probably harder than his record-breaking game against the New York Yanks. Still, Van Brocklin's show that night was a game to remember.

In 1971, Norm Van Brocklin was voted into the Pro Football Hall of Fame. There he took his place along with the Rams quarterback he had replaced—Bob Waterfield.

A lifetime of great football

Alive and Kicking!

The Houston Oilers played in the AFL (American Football League) in 1961. Their starting quarterback was George Blanda. He was 34 years old and had been playing pro football for 12 years.

At the start of the 1961 season, Houston fans were worried about Blanda. They thought he might be getting too old. He'd been outstanding in 1960. Still, no player could go on forever, especially a quarterback who also kicked field goals and extra points.

The Oilers lost three of their first five games. As a result, some sportswriters also started worrying about Blanda. They wondered if he should be starting at quarterback for Houston.

After their poor start, the Oilers played like champions. They ran off four wins in a row. Houston fans were thrilled. They couldn't wait to see their team try for win number five—against the New York Titans.

The Titans (later known as the Jets) had a winning record. They also had Al Dorow at quarterback. He'd led the AFL with 26 touchdown passes in 1960. The game was going to be a tough one.

The kickoff went to the Oilers. Cheering Houston fans watched their team march down the field. At the Titan 28-yard line, Blanda fired a perfect pass into the end zone for the first points of the game. Blanda kicked the extra point, giving the Oilers a 7–0 lead.

Blanda threw two more touchdown passes in the first quarter. Of course, he also kicked the extra points. His third extra-point kick was his fiftieth extra point.

The Titans scored on a pass early in the second quarter. Blanda answered that score with a 66-yard touchdown pass.

Again, he kicked the extra point, giving the Oilers a 28–6 lead.

The quarterback/kicker: George Blanda in motion

Houston's defense harassed the New York team. Time after time, the Oilers broke through the line and rushed the Titans' quarterback.

Just before the quarter ended, Blanda hit an open player with his fifth touchdown pass. Houston fans cheered their veteran quarterback. He'd just topped his league record of four touchdown passes in a game. And the game was only half over!

Blanda tossed another touchdown pass in the third quarter. He added his sixth extra-point kick, giving the Oilers a 42–6 lead.

Fans who had worried about Blanda were now cheering his every move. They loved being at a record-breaking game.

Halfway through the last quarter, George Blanda gave the fans another reason to cheer. He threw his seventh scoring pass to tie the NFL record for the most touchdown passes in a game. Once more, he kicked the extra point—his fifty-fourth in a row!

When George Blanda left the field, Houston fans stood and cheered. They had seen an old player in the best game of his life.

The Oilers won their fifth straight game, 49–13. For the day, Blanda hit on 20 of 32 passes for 418 yards gained. He passed or kicked for all the Houston points.

It was a *great* game. Yet it was far too soon to call the game the best in George Blanda's football career. In fact, it was really far too soon to call him old.

In 1961, George Blanda threw four or more touchdown passes in each of four games. He led the league with 36 touchdown throws. He also gained 3,330 yards with his passes.

As the years went on, Blanda just seemed to get better. For three years

17

(1963–65), he led the AFL in completed passes.

In 1967, George Blanda went over to the Oakland Raiders (now the Los Angeles Raiders). He was 40, but he still played like a young man. At the end of the season, he had the league scoring title with 116 points. In all, he kicked 20 field goals and 56 extra points.

Blanda kept playing. He seemed like Old Man River. He just kept rolling along.

During the 1970 season, the Raiders' starting quarterback got hurt. So old George Blanda came into the game. He was 43 years old, but no one could tell. He threw two scoring passes to lead the team to a win.

A few weeks later, the great George Blanda kicked a 52-yard field goal to give the Raiders another win. Two weeks after that, the Raiders won another game with a Blanda field goal!

By 1975, Blanda was playing with men who hadn't been born when he started as a pro. He *was* getting old. Still, he had some great games left in him.

One week, Oakland beat the Redskins when Blanda kicked an overtime field goal. A week later, the Raiders beat Atlanta in overtime. Again, Blanda kicked the winning field goal.

George Blanda played his last game that year. During his 26-season career, he scored a record 2,002 points. He also threw 236 touchdown passes.

In 1981, the Pro Football Hall of Fame honored George Blanda. They voted him into membership.

Blanda was alive and kicking for a long time. Throwing seven touchdown passes in one game may have gotten him into the Hall of Fame. He probably could have quit in 1961 and still have made the Hall. Instead, he played another lifetime of pro football.

The rookie saves the game

Running Hot in the Cold

Gale Sayers signed to play for the Chicago Bears in 1965. He came to them after attending the University of Kansas.

At Kansas, Sayers had starred in the backfield. Chicago fans figured he'd also become a star with the Bears. Yet they didn't expect Sayers to do much in his first year. He needed some time to get used to playing pro ball.

Gale Sayers listened, watched, and waited. He knew his turn would come. He got his first chance a few weeks into the season. The Bears were in a losing game against the Green Bay Packers.

George Halas, the Bears' coach, sent Sayers into the game. The Bears lost, but Sayers scored two touchdowns. One came on a 65-yard play.

Chicago fans quickly decided Gale Sayers was ready for pro ball. They loved his running style. He seemed to be as fast as any running back in the league—maybe faster.

As the weeks passed, Sayers thrilled Chicago fans. He scored on running plays. He scored on passes. He even scored on punt returns. He couldn't be stopped!

Gale Sayers quickly became a record-breaker. He topped the NFL record for touchdowns by a player in his rookie year.

On December 12, the San Francisco 49ers came to Chicago. On opening day, San Francisco had beaten the Bears 52–24. Now Chicago wanted to make up for that loss. So did most of the 46,000 football fans who filled Wrigley Field. They wanted Gale Sayers to give the 49ers a lesson in running.

The cold weather that day didn't bother the Bears. They were used to playing in bad weather in the Windy City. But the playing field did worry them. The ground was soft from rain, and running on a soft field was never easy.

Gale Sayers gave the field a big test early in the first quarter. He caught a short pass and raced off. The 49ers chased after him, but Sayers was too fast. He ran 80 yards for a touchdown.

In the second quarter, Sayers scored again on a run from San Francisco's 21-yard line. A little later, he made a 7-yard run for his third touchdown of the game.

Chicago fans cheered loudly as the first half ended. The Bears had a 27–13 lead, and Gale Sayers looked great.

"Did you forget we already beat these guys?" the San Francisco coach said at the half. "Stop the rookie, and we win again."

The 49ers went out for the second half. They knew they had a tough job to do. Stopping Sayers wasn't going to be easy.

Fans screamed with excitement when the Bears came out for the second half. They wanted their team to give the 49ers a beating. After all, the 49ers had crushed the Bears on opening day.

Shortly after the third quarter started, Sayers brought the fans to their feet. On a run over tackle, he spotted a big opening and turned on the speed.

The 49ers chased, but Sayers was too fast for them. He scored his fourth touchdown on a 50-yard run.

Minutes later, Sayers rushed for one yard and another touchdown. With five touchdowns, he was only one away from tying the NFL record.

The 49ers fought back. They scored another touchdown early in the fourth quarter. They were behind 40–20.

Still fired up, Chicago quickly made another touchdown. Suddenly the game seemed out of reach for the 49ers. They were too far behind.

Some fans headed for the exits. They'd had enough of the cold. Others sat still. They wanted to be around at the end to cheer Sayers. They also wanted to see if he would score again.

Failing to move the ball, the 49ers punted. Sayers took the kick at the Chicago 15-yard line. He shook off one 49er and picked up speed.

San Francisco players chased the Bears' rookie star. Sayers raced on, picking up blockers as he went. Suddenly he was out in the open! Seconds later, he crossed the goal line. He'd scored his sixth touchdown on an 85-yard return!

When the game ended, the Bears had a 61–20 win. Their rookie, Gale Sayers, had tied the NFL record for touchdowns in a game. He'd played a super game. Some people called him the greatest running back in NFL history.

Gale Sayers finished his first season with a record 22 touchdowns. No rookie in pro football history had ever scored more touchdowns. For a time, his 22 touchdowns also stood as the regular-season touchdown record.

The following year, Sayers led the NFL in rushing, with 1,231 yards. He averaged 5.4 yards a carry. He also led the league

Rookie Gale Sayers smiles after scoring six touchdowns in one game, tying the NFL record.

in kickoff returns, averaging 31.2 yards a carry.

Gale Sayers continued his great play for several years. Meanwhile, injuries started cutting back his playing time.

Finally, Sayers played his last game in 1971. He was still a young man, but his running days were over. Injuries had taken his speed away.

In 1977, Gale Sayers was voted into the Pro Football Hall of Fame. His turn had been short, but it had been great.

Two minutes, two touchdowns

Hard Fought, Hard Won

Johnny Unitas played college football at the University of Louisville. He started at quarterback and dreamed of playing pro football.

After graduation, Johnny Unitas wasn't able to sign with an NFL team for the season. So for the 1955 football season, he played quarterback on a small-town team in Pennsylvania. He was paid a few dollars for each game. It was better than playing for nothing, but not much better.

Early in 1956, Johnny got word of tryouts for the Baltimore (now Indianapolis) Colts. This time, Johnny Unitas made the team.

Soon after the season started, Unitas got to start at quarterback. He did well enough that day to become the Colts' regular quarterback for the rest of 1956.

Unitas turned into a star quarterback in 1957. He led the league in touchdown passes. He also led the Colts to their first winning season ever.

For the next three years (1958–60), Unitas led the NFL in touchdown passes. At the same time, he worked up a record that may never be broken. He threw for touchdowns in 47 straight games before missing one in 1960!

Year after year, Johnny Unitas continued throwing touchdown passes for the Colts. The 1967 season marked his twelfth year of throwing passes for Baltimore. Unitas was getting older. Yet he seemed to be getting better.

In September of 1967, Unitas passed for 401 yards against Atlanta. This was a new one-game record for him.

The Atlanta game pleased Unitas. He liked winning. For this reason, an upcoming November game with the Green

Bay Packers stuck in his mind. They'd beaten the Colts five games in a row!

The Colts and the Packers came to their game with top records. The Colts hadn't lost a game in 1967. The Packers had only one loss in seven games.

Over 60,000 fans filled Baltimore Memorial Stadium on November 5. The Packers were the defending champions of pro football. They'd won Super Bowl I.

Baltimore fans were proud of the Colts' record. Still, they feared the champion Packers. They always seemed to find a way to win.

Bart Starr played quarterback for Green Bay. In his years with the Packers, he'd thrown many touchdown passes. With Unitas and Starr playing, there was sure to be a lot of scoring.

Both teams surprised the crowd with shows of defense. When the first quarter ended, the score was 0–0.

The second quarter was another show of defense. The Packers got the only score—on a 49-yard field goal. At the half, they led 3–0.

Baltimore fans wanted action. They screamed for a score, but the Colts couldn't get moving. Neither could the Packers. After three quarters, the score stood at 3–0.

The game puzzled fans. They were watching two of the best quarterbacks in pro ball. Yet neither man had thrown one touchdown pass. It certainly wasn't the game the fans had expected.

Bart Starr changed matters early in the fourth quarter. He got off a 31-yard touchdown pass. The Packers fans cheered. The extra point was good. Green Bay led 10–0.

The kickoff went to Baltimore. Unitas tried hard, but the Packers defense stopped him again. The football went back to Green Bay. Colts fans booed.

The Packers were stopped, too. Johnny Unitas had another chance with about six minutes left to play. There was plenty of time to win—or at least tie.

Many sports fans believe the great players are best in the really tough games. Johnny Unitas started looking like he believed it, too. His passes moved the Colts up the field.

Seconds later, excited Baltimore fans jumped to their feet. A 10-yard Unitas pass gave the Colts a touchdown. The game wasn't over yet.

The excitement quickly ended. The Baltimore kicker missed the extra point. The score was 10–6. Now the Colts couldn't tie the game with a field goal. They needed another touchdown—or they would go down for their first loss of the season.

The clock showed about two minutes left to play. Unitas was hot now. Bart Starr could get hot, too. If he did, the Colts might not see the ball again. Or the Packers might score and put the game out of reach. Baltimore decided to try an onside kick.

Both teams charged after the kick. The football bounced off a Packer. A Colt jumped on it! Baltimore had the ball!

The Colts were in a good spot on the Packer 34-yard line. Two Unitas passes missed. A run gained four yards. It was fourth down for Baltimore.

Johnny Unitas, quarterback of the Baltimore Colts, looks out over the line as he calls the signals.

Unitas didn't pass. He ran—for a gain of seven yards. The Colts had a first down!

Unitas rolled back to pass. He spotted an open man and fired. The man scored! This time, the extra point was good. The Colts won 13–10!

In less than two minutes, Johnny Unitas had thrown two touchdown passes. He'd won the game for the Colts. Their fans stood and cheered. He was great!

Johnny Unitas retired at the end of 1973. In 18 years of pro play, he passed for over 40,000 yards. Six years later, he was given a well-deserved place in the Football Hall of Fame.

Namath promises and delivers

The Big Mouth's Big Game

Joe Namath was a star at quarterback for the University of Alabama. When he left college, the Cardinals tried to sign him for NFL play. The New York Jets of the AFL wanted him, too.

Namath decided on the Jets. He signed to play for them in 1965.

Namath started at quarterback and threw 18 touchdown passes in his first year of pro football. The Jets won only five games, but New York fans liked Joe Namath.

The fans enjoyed Namath's style. He was handsome, and he acted like a star—on and off the field. He made the news, playing football and hanging out in nightclubs. He seemed just right for New York City.

In 1966, Namath completed 232 passes, and the Jets won six games. After the season, the AFL championship winner played the NFL winner in Super Bowl I. The NFL won. The 1967 NFL champions also won Super Bowl II.

The Jets won eight games that season. Namath passed for a record 4,007 yards. He was becoming a superstar!

The Jets jumped to 11 wins in 1968. In the AFL championship game, Namath passed for three touchdowns. The Jets won! They were champions of the AFL!

The Baltimore (now Indianapolis) Colts easily won the NFL title, 34–0. Gamblers immediately made them huge favorites to win Super Bowl III.

Meanwhile, the owners of NFL and AFL teams had worked together. They planned to join the NFL and the AFL into one league by 1970. Making one league, the NFL, made sense. After all, the teams were already playing each other in Super Bowls.

Longtime NFL players didn't think much of the AFL. They thought the NFL was a much stronger league. They pointed to the past Super Bowl games for proof.

"Easy wins for us," NFL players said. "Our worst teams can beat the AFL winner."

Many sportswriters went to Miami to see the Colts and Jets in training. The writers hoped for some good stories.

The AFL title win made Namath a superstar. He had fame to go with his style. He also had a habit of making the news. Writers hung around him, trying to get Joe Namath to say something big. They also kept reminding him about how tough the Colts would be.

Finally, Namath had heard enough. "We'll beat the Colts," he said. "I *guarantee* we'll win."

As expected, Namath made the news. Some NFL players sneered at what he'd said. "He's a big mouth," they said. "On Sunday, he'll get to eat his words."

Over 75,000 football fans filled Miami's Orange Bowl for Super Bowl III. Many came to see the Jets get beat. Others came to see the Jets' super quarterback teach the Colts some new football tricks.

Namath's big talk fired up the Jets. They kept the hard-hitting Colts away from him. On defense, they stopped Baltimore's passing and running games. After one quarter, the score was 0–0.

Namath (left) tucks the ball into the arms of running back Bill Mathis.

Broadway Joe drops back to pass. The New York Jets went on to beat the Baltimore Colts, 16–7.

No score, but the Jets were on the move. NFL teams hadn't been able to run against the Colts all year. But Namath just kept calling for running plays.

Surprised by Namath's calls, the Colts made mistakes and gave up yards. Namath switched back to passing. Three completions carried the Jets to the Baltimore 9-yard line.

Again, Joe Namath called for running plays. Two plays later, a Jet back ran wide for a touchdown. The extra point was good, giving the Jets a 7–0 lead.

For the rest of the quarter, the Colts looked bad. They made more mistakes. They weren't playing like huge favorites. Still, the game was far from over. Baltimore fans figured the Colts would get rolling soon.

A field goal early in the second half gave the Jets another score. Minutes later, Namath's passes moved them into field-goal position again. A 30-yard kick pushed the Jets' lead to 13–0.

The game moved into the last quarter. Again, Namath moved the Jets down the field. Another New York field goal put the score at 16–0.

Some Baltimore fans still believed their team could win. Johnny Unitas had come in at quarterback for the Colts. The old star had saved games before. He could do it again.

Unitas thrilled Baltimore fans. He led the Colts up the field to the Jets' 1-yard line. The Baltimore fullback bulled his way over for a touchdown. The extra point was good. The score was 16–7, but time was running out.

Namath took over. By calling running plays, he kept the ball from the Colts. The Jets won 16–7. They'd scored the biggest upset in pro football history. Namath had talked big—and played big.

After the game, Namath was named Most Valuable Player. He'd led his team to a super Super Bowl win.

The NFL and AFL came together as one league soon after that win by the Jets. Of course, Joe Namath then became an NFL star. Though he had bad knees, he kept playing through 1977.

Joe Namath was elected to the Pro Football Hall of Fame in 1985. He still had his special style. He'd become a national celebrity.

The NFL's longest field goal

Doing the Impossible

Tom Dempsey was born with no right hand and only half a right foot. His parents probably didn't think he'd become a pro football player some day.

As Dempsey grew up, he was often encouraged to try things—even if they seemed hard. By the time he reached high school, he was big and strong. He liked football, so he tried out for the team.

To the surprise of many, Tom Dempsey made his high school football team. He played tackle. On his half of a foot, he wore a shoe that was cut off and sewn back together. Kids who played against Dempsey quickly learned about him. The kid with the funny shoe and no right hand could play football.

Dempsey went on to junior college. There he taped the front of his special shoe and started kicking field goals and extra points.

In 1967, Dempsey played for a team in the Atlantic Coast Football League. It wasn't the NFL, but it was still a lot tougher than junior college.

The following year, Dempsey signed with the San Diego Chargers. He didn't make the team, but they kept him on for the practice season. Meanwhile, Dempsey had a special kicking shoe made. The leather on the front of it was much better than tape.

In the summer, the Chargers dropped Dempsey. But he wasn't through. He wanted to play pro football. In 1969 he signed with the New Orleans Saints. He'd made the NFL!

Tom Dempsey kicked 22 field goals in his first season with the Saints. In all, the rookie kicker scored 99 points in 1969. When the season was over, he played in the NFL Pro Bowl. He'd come a long way in one year.

New Orleans played terribly in 1970. Halfway through the season, the Saints had one win, five losses, and one tie. Some fans wondered if they were ever going to win another game.

Tom Dempsey was having his troubles, too. He'd made 5 of 15 field goals. The Saints had a new coach. Dempsey hoped the coach wasn't looking for a new kicker.

Bad team or not, the people of New Orleans liked football. Over 65,000 fans came out on November 8, 1970. Most of them expected the Detroit Lions to chew up the Saints. Some hoped for the impossible—a New Orleans win.

Dempsey kicked a 29-yard field goal in the first quarter. New Orleans fans cheered. Their Saints were leading 3–0.

The Lions fought back. They scored a touchdown in the second quarter. With the extra point, Detroit led 7–3.

The Saints continued to surprise their fans. They moved up the field once more.

When they got close enough, they let Dempsey kick again. This time, he scored with a 27-yard field goal. At the half, Detroit led 7–6.

In the third quarter, the Lions scored on a short pass. They added the extra point and jumped ahead 14–6.

Battling back, the Saints got inside the Detroit 10-yard line. Still, they couldn't score a touchdown. Tom Dempsey came out and kicked his third field goal of the game. Detroit led 14–9.

New Orleans finally scored a touchdown. It came on a run in the fourth quarter. Dempsey added the extra point, giving the Saints a 16–14 lead.

New Orleans fans cheered. Time was running out. The Saints could win the game!

The cheering quickly ended. Detroit rolled up the field. By the time New Orleans stopped them, the Lions were in position for a field goal. They decided to go for it. The 18-yard kick went up. It was good! Detroit led 17–16!

The clock showed 11 seconds left. The miracle win seemed lost. Still, some time was better than no time.

After the kickoff, the Saints tried a pass. The man who caught it stepped outside. He hadn't reached midfield and the clock showed two seconds left.

Tom Dempsey came into the game. He was going to try for a field goal. It was impossible. He was too far away. Some fans figured he would fake a field goal and then pass. Other fans just started for home.

The ball was snapped. Tom Dempsey kicked from 63 yards out. The ball sailed through the air. The signal was made. The kick was good! The game was over! The Saints had won 19–17!

Dempsey was thrilled. He also had waited for the signal. He was so far away he couldn't see whether the kick got there. His teammates jumped all over him. They were overjoyed. So were the fans. They almost couldn't believe their eyes. Tom Dempsey had done the impossible.

The last-second scoring kick gave the Saints their second win of the season. In a

Dempsey makes the kick that put him in the record books—a 63-yard field goal against Detroit.

way, the win was a miracle. It was New Orleans' last win in 1970.

Tom Dempsey played in the NFL for several more years. He kicked some other long field goals, too. Of course, he never

47

Fans and teammates lift Dempsey up, celebrating his new record and the New Orleans win.

kicked another 63-yard field goal. That kick put Tom Dempsey in the NFL record book. After more than 20 years, his kick is still the longest ever.

Payton breaks O. J.'s record

The Running Machine

Walter Payton starred in college football at Jackson State University. As a running back at the Mississippi school, Payton gained over 3,500 yards. Pro teams wanted him. The Chicago Bears made him their number one pick. Payton signed to play with the Bears in 1975.

Payton rushed for seven touchdowns in his first year with the Bears. This didn't make him a star, but Chicago fans liked his play. They really liked the way he returned kickoffs. In fact, he led the league with an average of 31.7 yards on 14 tries.

Walter Payton ran a lot more in his second year. His 311 rushes topped the league. He gained 1,390 yards rushing and scored 13 touchdowns.

After the 1976 season, Payton was picked to play in his first Pro Bowl. The young man from Mississippi had quickly become a top player. Still, he wasn't the best rusher in pro football. That title belonged to O. J. Simpson, the Buffalo Bills star.

Simpson had set many records in his eight years of pro football. In 1976, he'd rushed for a new record of 273 yards in a game against Detroit. The old record of 250 yards that he broke was set in 1973—by O. J. Simpson.

Walter Payton admired O. J. Simpson. Yet Payton's mind wasn't on Simpson's records when the 1977 season started. Payton wanted the Bears to win a championship. He wanted his team to play in a Super Bowl.

In game after game, the Bears called on Payton to get them the yards they needed. Payton was the team's workhorse. After nine games, he was leading the league in rushing attempts. He was also leading the league with 1,129 yards gained rushing.

On November 20, 1977, close to 50,000 fans came out to see the hometown Bears go against the Minnesota Vikings. Minnesota was in first place. They'd beaten the Bears in an overtime game in October. The Vikings were favored to win again.

Chicago fans knew Walter Payton had been sick all week. They'd read about his battle with the flu in the newspapers. Still, he was going to play. Some fans worried he wasn't ready for the Vikings.

The first quarter ended in a 0–0 tie. In the second quarter, a 1-yard run by Payton broke the tie. His touchdown and the extra point gave the Bears a 7–0 lead.

Before the second quarter was over, the Bears scored a field goal. That gave them a 10–0 halftime lead. During the first half, Walter Payton carried the ball 26 times and gained 144 yards.

The Vikings weren't through. They scored a touchdown in the third quarter. The Bears failed to score. They led 10–7 at the end of the quarter.

By now, Chicago fans had forgotten all about Payton's flu. The Vikings' front line was tough, but Payton was tough, too. He picked up yards almost every time he carried the ball.

Every time Minnesota got the ball, they were stopped by the Bears. Finally, Payton passed the 200-yard mark in rushing. It was the second time that year he'd gone over 200 yards rushing in one game.

Near the end of the quarter, Payton made a long run down the sideline. The run gave him 268 yards in the game.

Walter Payton was close to O. J. Simpson's one-game rushing record. Yet the record still wasn't on Payton's mind. It wasn't on the minds of the other Bears, either. The game was too close to worry about breaking records.

"Give the ball to Payton!" Chicago fans yelled.

The fans weren't thinking about Simpson's record, either. They were thinking about getting more points. They were also thinking about keeping the ball from the Vikings.

Payton rushed again and gained three yards. On his next rush, he made four

Payton gains yards in the game against the Vikings. He set the one-game rushing record with 275 yards.

yards. His total for the game stood at 275 yards. He had broken the record for rushing in one game! He'd broken O. J. Simpson's record.

Neither team scored in the fourth quarter. So the Bears won 10–7. They had upset the Vikings! Chicago fans cheered their team and the record-breaking running of Walter Payton.

After 10 games, Payton had 1,404 yards gained rushing. He had four games left to play. The one-season record for rushing was 2,003 yards. O. J. Simpson held that record, too. Some fans thought Walter Payton might set a new record.

Winning was more important to Payton than setting records. In fact, he gave the Chicago offensive line all the credit for his 275-yard rushing game. "They made the openings," he said.

In the end, Payton rushed for 1,852 yards in 1977. Of course, he led the league. He also led the league with 14 touchdowns scored by rushing.

The Bears finally got into a Super Bowl after the 1985 season. Luckily, they still had their great running back Walter Payton. In Super Bowl XX, Payton gained 61 yards. Chicago beat New England 46–10. Walter Payton had the championship win he'd always wanted.

Payton played pro football through 1987. In all, he rushed for an NFL record of 16,726 yards. He also scored 125 touchdowns during his pro playing days.

From the beginning, the Chicago Bears expected a lot from Walter Payton. Still, he gave them more than they expected. He became one of the greatest running backs in NFL history. In 1993, Walter Payton was elected to the Pro Football Hall of Fame.

Passing without fail

Super Bowl Superman

Joe Montana was Notre Dame's quarterback. In 1979, he signed with the San Francisco 49ers. He became their regular quarterback in 1980.

From the beginning, Montana showed he could spot open men and pass the ball to them. After the 1981 season, he led San Francisco to victory in Super Bowl XVI. The 49ers beat Cincinnati 26–21. Following the game, Joe Montana was named Most Valuable Player.

The 49ers got back into Super Bowl play after the 1984 season. This time, San Francisco met Miami in Super Bowl XIX.

Once again, Montana led the 49ers. He passed for 331 yards. He threw three touchdown passes and ran for another touchdown. San Francisco won 38–16. The 49ers won another NFL title!

The Super Bowl Most Valuable Player title went to Joe Montana for a second time. In six years of pro play, Montana had become an outstanding quarterback.

Montana continued his great passing. In 1987, he led the NFL with 31 touchdown passes. During the season, he set a league record when he completed 22 passes in a row. This record was set over two games (5 in the first game, and 17 in the second).

Following the 1988 season, Super Bowl XXIII matched the 49ers against the Cincinnati Bengals. The game promised to be a tough battle for both teams.

Over 75,000 people filled Joe Robbie Stadium in Miami for Super Bowl XXIII. Millions more watched the game on TV.

Both teams fought hard from the opening kickoff. After 10 minutes of play, the score stood at 0–0. The 49ers kicked a field goal minutes later. At the end of the quarter, San Francisco led 3–0.

The second quarter turned into another battle of defense. With less than two minutes left, neither team had scored in the quarter. Seconds later, the Bengals kicked a field goal. At halftime, the game was tied 3–3.

The second-half kickoff went to Cincinnati. The Bengals slowly worked their way up the field. Still, they couldn't get a touchdown. Another Cincinnati field goal put them ahead 6–3.

A 49er field goal tied the score at 6–6. The clock showed less than a minute left in the third quarter.

With fans wondering if they were going to see a touchdown in the game, San Francisco kicked off. Suddenly, the fans were on their feet! The Bengals had scored the game's first touchdown on a 93-yard kickoff return. The extra point was good. The Bengals led 13–6 at the end of the third quarter.

Joe Montana opened the fourth quarter with a completed pass. The pass was good

Joe Montana, the star quarterback of the 49ers

for 40 yards. Excited San Francisco fans cheered. Their team was on the Bengals 14-yard line.

Two plays later, Montana fired off his first touchdown pass of the game. The extra point tied the score at 13–13.

The tight battle continued. Cincinnati failed to score. San Francisco also failed to score. The Bengals got ready to try to break the tie.

Cincinnati pushed up the field. Still, they couldn't break loose for a touchdown. They settled for another field goal. With a little over three minutes left in the game, the Bengals led 16–13.

San Francisco fans wanted magic from Montana. A penalty on the kickoff put the 49ers on their own 8-yard line.

Joe Montana passed for eight yards. He followed with two more completed passes. They were short passes. A running play gained only one yard. The two-minute warning stopped the clock.

Another running play gave San Francisco four more yards. Montana fired off a 17-yard pass. Montana's next pass was good for 13 yards. The 49ers were coming into range for a field goal. Still, a field goal would only tie the score.

Three plays later, Montana hit on a 27-yard pass. Another completed pass followed. The pass was good for another eight yards. Montana had gotten the 49ers to the Bengals' 10-yard line. The clock showed only 39 seconds left to play in Super Bowl XXIII.

On the very next play, Joe Montana fired a touchdown pass! With the extra point, San Francisco had a four-point lead over Cincinnati. The Bengals needed a touchdown, but they only had about 30 seconds left to play.

In the end, the 49ers held their lead and won 20–16. Joe Montana, the Superman of Super Bowls, had gotten his team to another championship!

For the game, the Most Valuable Player award went to Jerry Rice of the 49ers. Rice, a wide receiver, caught 11 passes from Montana. In all, Rice set a Super Bowl record by gaining 215 yards on those passes.

Joe Montana also set a Super Bowl record. He passed for 357 yards in the game. No passer in Super Bowl history had ever thrown for more yards.

The following year, Joe Montana proved to be a Superman once more. He led the 49ers to a 55–10 Super Bowl win over Denver. He also won his third Most Valuable Player award.

Montana threw five touchdown passes against Denver. His touchdown passing set another Super Bowl record. No doubt, Joe Montana will go into the Pro Football Hall of Fame. He can't miss!

Montana lets out a yell of victory as he leaves the field. The 49ers won the Super Bowl, 20–16.